GOD

Hearing

GOD

FOR INTIMACY, HEALING, CREATIVITY, MEDITATION, AND DREAM INTERPRETATION

MARK & PATTI VIRKLER

DESTINY IMAGE® PUBLISHERS, INC.
P.O. Box 310, Shippensburg, PA 17257-0310
"Promoting Inspired Lives."

This book and all other Destiny Image and Destiny Image Fiction books are available at Christian bookstores and distributors worldwide.

Cover Design by: Prodigy Pixel

For more information on foreign distributors, call 717-532-3040.
Reach us on the Internet: www.destinyimage.com.

ISBN 13 TP: 978-0-7684-0511-8
ISBN 13 Ebook: 978-0-7684-0512-5

For Worldwide Distribution, Printed in the U.S.A.
2 3 4 5 6 7 8 / 18 17 16 15

CONTENTS

INTRODUCTION

*Draw near to God and He will
draw near to you* (James 4:8).

CHRISTIANITY IS UNIQUE AMONG RELIGIONS. IT ALONE OFFERS a personal relationship with the Creator beginning here and now and lasting throughout eternity. Truly, God Himself has given both you and I the ultimate invitation. Because of Jesus's work, we are able to hear, know, and enjoy a lifestyle of communion with an interactive, living God.

We do not embrace a "clockmaker" approach to life, where we acknowledge some deity who initiated the created order but then stepped back, allowing things to take their natural course. Throughout history, the Creator has demonstrated the exact opposite desire—culminating with the redemptive work

of Calvary. Jesus died—yes, to cleanse humankind of sin, but also to remove the barriers preventing constant communion between Heaven and earth.

Jesus declared, *"This is eternal life, that they may know You, the only true God"* (John 17:3, emphasis added). Unfortunately, many in the Church miss the great blessing of fellowship with our Lord because we have lost the ability to recognize His voice within us. The work has already been accomplished. Everything that needed to be done in order for you and I to *hear God* has already been finished. Now it is a quest of rediscovery. This is why I wanted to share this project with you.

It is unique. In fact, it is something that I have long wanted to do, as my vision is to help the body of Christ *hear* again. So I invite you to join me on an interactive journey to hearing God. More than a book of teaching, this project is more an outlet for *your* interaction with God. I am going to share some teaching throughout, but more than anything I want to help you make space in your own life to hear from God. He longs to speak to you!

That is exactly what this journal has been designed to facilitate. This is not a strict, "it has to be *this way*" approach. My only request is that you would consider the keys and principles shared and ask the Holy Spirit to show you how to incorporate them into your personal fellowship with God.

Don't strain. Remember, the great chasm of sin has been removed, which means you already have access to hear from God. However, many of us miss His voice simply because we do not know how to practically recognize it. The following pages are all about helping you tune in to the One who is constantly speaking.

Introduction

This journal is divided up into *three sections*, with each section theme building on the previous one.

BREAKDOWN

First, we are going to review the *4 Keys to Hearing God's Voice*. These are the foundational building blocks to your communion with God. Though we have the promise that "My sheep hear My voice" (John 10:27), too many believers are starved for that intimate relationship with the Father that alone can satisfy the desire of their hearts. I was one of those sheep who was deaf to his Shepherd until the Lord revealed four very simple keys (found in Habakkuk 2:1-2) that unlocked the treasure of His voice.

Second, we are going to explore what it looks like to *Meditate on God's Voice*. Once we discover how easy it is to hear God's voice, the question is, "Now what?" Meditation follows hearing. Remember what Jesus said about those who *hear* but do not *act* on what they hear? The process of hearing from God is incomplete unless we act upon what we hear. This is not a summons to religious busyness. For what we are focusing on in these pages, the *action* is meditation. Before there is manifestation, I believe there must be meditation. Our minds must be transformed before we go out and change the world around us. Otherwise, we are just shooting in the dark or trying to follow some type of religious system. I will give you a practical, seven-step process on *How to Meditate on a Topic* that is simply designed to help you practice biblical meditation in your everyday life. We must demystify meditation in order to enjoy its wonderful benefits.

Third—and perhaps the most misunderstood way that God communicates—I want us to look at *Hearing God through Our Dreams*. When you recognize the 4 Keys to hearing God's voice and develop a lifestyle of meditating on what He is saying, your dream life will increase in activity. Biblical meditation is a powerful catalyst to experiencing God speaking to you in the night through dreams, as His Word constantly fills your mind and heart. We must learn how to be aware of what God is saying, consistently record our dreams, and pray for discernment and interpretation.

Each section will be introduced by a brief segment of teaching and then will be followed by plenty of writing space for you to interact with God yourself.

HOW TO ENGAGE

Here is how I recommend you engage the following pages:

1. **Sections:** I have broken the book up into three sections, simply to help you identify which unique subjects you will be covering.

2. **Entries:** The book is not broken up into specific days/weeks, as I want you to go through this journey at your own pace. However, I do recommend you go through *one entry per day* to get the most out of your experience. Most importantly, I want you to use this journal in a way that makes the most sense to your personal walk with the Lord. Freely skip to a section of maximum relevance if need be. For example, if you have a vivid dream one night and want to record it, I encourage you

to write it down in the appropriate area in Section Three. There is lined space for recording seven sample dreams. Likewise, if there is a specific verse you have on your heart that you would like to meditate on, go directly to Section Two on *Biblical Meditation*.

3. **"Hearing God in Everyday Life" Stories:** Throughout this journal, I am also including stories and testimonies of those who have heard God in one of the different ways we are discussing and how hearing His voice transformed their lives, ushering them into healing, creativity, and breakthrough.

FOUR KEYS TO HEARING GOD'S VOICE

My sheep hear My voice (John 10:27).

*For as many as are led by the Spirit of God,
these are sons of God* (Romans 8:14).

My Sheep *Really Do* Hear My Voice!

Introducing the 4 Keys to Hearing God's Voice

I tossed and turned in bed, unable to fall asleep. The thought kept going through my mind: "What if I died tonight? I'm not ready to go to Heaven." I could not shake the thought, so I got up, went downstairs, and waited for my parents to come home from their meeting. When they did, I announced that I wanted to get saved, and they took me straightway to the pastor's home where he explained the plan of salvation and led me in the sinner's prayer. I was 15 years old when I accepted Jesus Christ into my heart as my Lord and Savior.

It was God's voice that was speaking to me that night, calling me into His kingdom. His voice came as a spontaneous thought inside my head. However, I didn't define this as the primary way God's voice is heard until I had completed a desperate 10-year search to hear Him clearly.

Unfortunately, many in the Church live in that place of straining and struggling to hear God speak. They miss the great blessing of fellowship with our Lord because we have lost the ability to recognize His voice. Though John 10:27 promises us that "My sheep hear My voice," too many believers are starved for that intimate relationship that alone can satisfy the desire of their hearts.

I was one of those sheep who was unable to identify the voice of my Shepherd. I hungered for deeper spiritual intimacy with God, but I could not find it. Then on the eleventh year of my Christian life, I had the spontaneous thought, "I should take a year of my life and focus on learning how to hear God's voice." I decided to act on that thought and devote a year to a focused effort—learning to hear His voice. Unbeknownst to me, it was the Lord Himself calling me to invest that time.

That year the Lord revealed four simple keys, all found in Habakkuk 2:1-2, which unlocked the treasure of His voice. Using the 4 Keys together allowed me to easily hear God's voice on a daily basis. It was the most transforming step I have taken in the 45 years of my Christian life! I would like to share them with you so you can try them and watch as they open your ears to hearing God like never before.

Key #1

*God's voice in your heart often sounds
like a flow of spontaneous thoughts.*

You Can Be Confident That God Is Speaking to You

*Then the Lord answered me and
said…* (Habakkuk 2:2).

The prophet Habakkuk knew the sound of God speaking to him.

- It was clear.

- It was familiar.

- It was recognizable.

As you set out on this journey, pause and consider how clearly you are currently hearing God's voice speaking to you.

In what ways do you sense that God currently speaks to you?

5-24-15 God spoke as I was lying in my Bed with aches on my body, told me to speak the word to my and you shall be healed

When was the last time that you clearly heard God's voice?

In a dream, I was saying thanks you Jesus Hallelujah, when I saw a cherub- stand w/ me hold my hands and said the same thing

If you believe that you are currently not hearing God's voice or it has been a long time since you last heard God speaking to you, prepare for a transition. *You can be confident that God is speaking to you*, just as Habakkuk was.

Trust the Lord that soon you will be able to use the same confident language that the prophet of old did—*Then the Lord answered me and said....*

Spend a few moments in prayer. Write down what you are asking God to do in your life during this journey into hearing God's voice. Be bold, and remember that the Father in Heaven wants you to hear His voice even more than you want to hear His voice!

About my family, about myself, why is there a blockage whenever I ask about my teeth my finance, my health I would like to help young women, a place of respite for them to reconize their purpose, about my marriage what is going on, my food ministry, I want to get started about my mind, how can I focus on the Lord, and do the things He wants me to do about remembering, things. having your unconditional love, letting go and letting you have your way in my life

interpreting my dreams
knowledge, wisdom, understanding
Showing me my disobedience
my lack of Trust in you
my unbelieve. Doubts and
fears, removing all anxiety,
Lack of Trust for others,

LEARN TO RECOGNIZE
THE STILL SMALL VOICE

*…and after the fire a still small
voice* (1 Kings 19:12).

GOD SPOKE TO THE PROPHET ELIJAH IN A *STILL SMALL
voice*. He was able to recognize that, in this instance, God was
not speaking in dramatic ways such as fire, an earthquake, or
wind. Just like Elijah was able to clearly recognize the speaking
voice of God, *you too* can confidently know when and how God
is speaking to you.

Remember, Elijah was a human being just like you and I
(see James 5:17-18). If he could discern the still small voice of
God, so can you!

What do you think the "still small voice of God" sounds like?

It speaks to your spirit, in your mind

Have you ever heard God speaking to you in this way? What did it sound like?

Someone talking in your ~~ears~~ Spirit through your ears

This *still small voice* is not an audible voice that you hear with your natural ears—at least not normally. Rather, it is what Paul describes in Romans 8:16, where he talks about how the *"Spirit Himself bears witness with our spirit that we are children of God."* The Holy Spirit bears witness in your spirit concerning truth. Most important, He gives you an internal assurance that you are born again and that you are a child of God.

This is one of the principal ways that God communicates with His people—through His Spirit bearing witness with your spirit.

Ask the Holy Spirit to give you specific words to describe the process of how He "bears witness" with your spirit. Write this down and review your description. Can you think of some recent examples in your life where you experienced God speaking to you this way?

take my guitar and go
Sing for the Elderly, and
call it a sing-A-long
Cook some food, Bless The church

GOD SPEAKS THROUGH YOUR SPONTANEOUS THOUGHTS

But as it is written: "Eye has not seen, nor ear heard, nor have entered into the heart of man the things which God has prepared for those who love Him." But God has revealed them to us through His Spirit (1 Corinthians 2:9-10).

HAVE YOU EVER BEEN IN A SITUATION WHERE, AS YOU WENT along with your normal day, a specific thought came to your mind—a thought that compelled you to pray? Maybe it was for a certain person or a particular situation.

We may not recognize it immediately, but those seemingly spontaneous thoughts are vehicles through which God speaks to us. In these instances, God is speaking to you by sharing His own thoughts with you.

What do these spontaneous thoughts look like to you? Have you experienced this in your Christian life?

Like get up now go help someone
Pick up the Bible and read
scriptures and pray

In the last three days, have any of these spontaneous thoughts come to your mind?

In the Old Covenant, the thoughts of God were a mystery (see Isa. 55:8-9). In the New Covenant, we are given the opportunity to actually know the thoughts of God as the Holy Spirit reveals them to us. When you experience spontaneous thoughts that lead you to pray, be confident that God is at work. He is speaking to you. He is inviting you to know His thoughts and actually partner with Him in praying for His will and His purposes over what He is revealing to you.

Pause and pray. Perhaps God wants to reveal His thoughts to you in this moment. Write down any spontaneous thoughts that come to your mind about specific people or situations that you could pray for.

My children love the Lord and he is working on them, they are allowing to cares of this life to hinder their Blessings, how God healed me today,

SPIRIT-LEVEL COMMUNICATION

But if they are prophets, and if the word of the Lord is with them, let them now make intercession to the Lord of hosts (Jeremiah 27:18).

EXPERIENCE INDICATES THAT WE OFTEN PERCEIVE SPIRIT-LEVEL communication as spontaneous thoughts, impressions, and visions. One definition of *paga*, which is the Hebrew word for intercession, is "a chance encounter or accidental intersecting."

This passage from Jeremiah represents a summons for the authentic prophets of God to stand in the gap and pray on behalf of the *"vessels which are left in the house of the Lord."* Through intercession, God uses "accidental intersections" and invites us

to pray on behalf of someone else, serving as a "go-between." We simply need to start recognizing that He speaks this way, rather than discounting the thoughts as arbitrary, random, or unimportant.

Is there anyone God is "intersecting your path with" today? Make a list of any people who seem to be coming up in *spontaneous thoughts*.

You might want to make this list on a separate document in your phone, tablet, computer, etc. so it will be easily accessible to you.

Joy, my sister's son wife and children, Bro David

Pray over each name on your list. Ask the Holy Spirit to give you wisdom, direction, and specifics as you pray for them.

Your so-called "chance encounters" are actually divinely orchestrated setups by a God who sees and knows all. He is not only speaking to you, but He is inviting you into His purposes by using your voice and your intercession as His method for bringing His plans to pass. You get to play a role in the process as one who hears God's voice and releases His words!

Continue to add to this prayer list. Live mindful that God will communicate with you through seemingly spontaneous thoughts. Ask the Holy Spirit to help you immediately recognize when He is speaking and train you to pause, listen, and pray.

Key #2

Become still so you can sense
God's flow of thoughts.

BE STILL AND LISTEN

I will [in my thinking] stand upon my post of observation and station myself on the tower or fortress, and will watch to see what He will say within me (Habakkuk 2:1 AMP).

THE PROPHET HABAKKUK KNEW THAT IN ORDER TO HEAR God's quiet, inner, spontaneous thoughts, he had to first go to a quiet place and still his own thoughts and emotions. Reflect on the language he uses. To Habakkuk, being still meant a resolution of thought. He had to make an effort to be still. Doesn't this make sense in our extremely fast-paced society today? Decide today that you will be still before the Lord and incline your heart to listen to His voice.

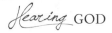

In order to meditate on the words of God (which we will look at in greater depth later on in our journey together), we must first resolve to *hear* what God is speaking. Habakkuk resolved to focus every part of his being—particularly his mind—to listening to what God was going to say to Him. This involves intentionally *becoming still.*

Over the next few days, I want to help you become quiet before the Lord and start to hear His voice. This does not mean we empty our minds and go blank. That is how the counterfeit works—eastern meditation. To listen to God is to wait quietly before Him as He longs to *fill* our minds with His thoughts and His Word.

If you had to evaluate the time you spent communicating with God, how much of it could be described as "being still"?

_____

_____

_____

_____

_____

_____

If you would honestly say that most of your time with God involves you speaking, get ready for a paradigm change as the Holy Spirit gently leads you on this journey to becoming still and hearing His voice.

Remember, His is often a still, small voice. In order to hear it, we likewise need to grow still.

_____

_____

_____

_____

_____

_____

_____

_____

_____

_____

_____

_____

_____

_____

_____

_____

_____

WAIT TO HEAR GOD'S VOICE

My soul, wait silently for God alone, for my expectation is from Him (Psalms 62:5).

When it comes to prayer, do you talk or listen more?

I listen Sometimes

Pause and honestly evaluate. If you tend to talk more, take this opportunity to pause, get still/silent before the Lord, and posture your heart in a place of expectation.

Write down what the Holy Spirit begins to share with you.

(Note any spontaneous/flowing thoughts that come to your mind.)

WRITE DOWN
GOD'S THOUGHTS

Truly my soul silently waits for God (Psalms 62:1).

THERE IS A DEEP INNER KNOWING (SPONTANEOUS FLOW) IN our spirits that each of us can experience when we quiet our flesh and our mind. If we are not still, we will sense only our own thoughts. However, when we quiet ourselves and set our expectation to hear from God, then we will not be tempted to simply hear our own thoughts.

Spend some time in silent waiting before God. What thoughts are coming to your mind? List them down in the space below.

_____

_____

_____

_____

_____

_____

_____

_____

_____

_____

_____

_____

_____

_____

_____

_____

Now evaluate the different thoughts that you listed. One tell-tale sign that the thoughts are from God is that they are in alignment with what is already written in Scripture. God will never violate His Word. What He says to you will always reflect His nature and character as revealed throughout Scripture.

WORSHIP: A GATEWAY TO HEARING GOD

*Then it happened, when the musician
played, that the hand of the Lord
came upon him* (2 Kings 3:15).

LOVING GOD THROUGH A QUIET WORSHIP SONG IS ONE VERY effective way to become still. This is *not* a formula designed to lock you into a method. In other words, there are times when God invites you into silence where a worship song might be disruptive. Allow your spirit to identify whether or not this is the right tool at the right time.

Scripture consistently reveals that worship is a gateway to God's presence. When God comes, He speaks to His people.

Also, a worship song helps reorient our minds to focus exclusively on Him. It is a catalyst that pushes distractions to the side and allows us to gaze upon His beauty.

After I worship and become silent within, I open myself for that spontaneous flow.

Find a quiet worship song and start to play it. Ask the Holy Spirit to direct your focus and attention on the true object of your worship—the Father.

As you worship, have ears ready to hear the voice of the Holy Spirit.

- He may speak to you directly through the song.
- He may cause you to write down some of the words and reflect on them.
- He may invite you to look up Scripture passages that the lyrics are based upon.

Write down what the Holy Spirit says to you through the worship experience.

_____

_____

_____

_____

_____

_____

THE ENEMY OF STILLNESS

When the enemy comes in like a flood,
the Spirit of the Lord will lift up a
standard against him (Isaiah 59:19).

WHILE YOU ARE INTENTIONALLY SETTING YOURSELF TO HEAR God's voice, be aware that the enemy will try to come in like a flood with distracting thoughts. First, *celebrate this*. Even though the devil is an annoyance and a nuisance, he is coming against you because he recognizes the value of your journey to hearing God's voice. The very fact that he is coming against you—and it often feels like a flood—means that you are breaking significant spiritual ground!

Pause a moment and reflect.

What thoughts tend to distract you from growing quiet before God and listening to His voice? (Examples: condemnation, worry, daily tasks, unworthiness, etc.)

Practical Tools to Overcome Distractions and Hear God Speak

Let us therefore come boldly to the throne of grace, that we may obtain mercy and find grace to help in time of need (Hebrews 4:16).

THE MOST CONSISTENT THOUGHTS THE ENEMY USES TO DIStract you from hearing God's voice are ones of sin, condemnation, and unworthiness. He wants you to feel guilty and thus unable to come before God's throne with boldness. This is a deception, and you have a scriptural right to come against every one of his lies!

If thoughts of guilt or unworthiness come against you, simply repent, receive the washing of the blood of the Lamb, and imagine yourself putting on Jesus's robe of righteousness. This is truly what enables us to stand spotless before the Holy God.

Find Scriptures to declare against the deceptions and lies of the enemy.

Here are some example Scriptures that equip you to stand against the enemy's lies of unworthiness and shame:

> *I will greatly rejoice in the Lord, my soul shall be joyful in my God; for He has clothed me with the garments of salvation, He has covered me with the robe of righteousness* (Isaiah 61:10).
>
> *And you, who once were alienated and enemies in your mind by wicked works, yet now He has reconciled in the body of His flesh through death, to present you holy, and blameless, and above reproach in His sight* (Colossians 1:21-22).
>
> *And they overcame him by the blood of the Lamb and by the word of their testimony* (Revelation 12:11).

Reflect for a moment on what lies the enemy uses to try to distract you from hearing God's voice. Ask the Holy Spirit to lead you to certain Scripture passages that arm you with truth to speak back against him.

Write these down!

Practical Tools to Overcome Distractions and Hear God Speak

Keep a Notebook Handy to Write Down "Other Things"

As you spend time learning how to posture your heart to be still before God, you will find that your mind will start running toward different tasks you need to perform, errands you need to run, or other tasks you need to be mindful of.

If thoughts come of things you have forgotten to do or need to do, write them down so you can do them later. Don't worry about this disrupting the flow of you hearing from God. In fact, it is very helpful to write these things down and "shelve" them for later. Once you record them, most likely they will leave your mind and keep you in a place where you can hear the still voice of God speaking to you.

Keep a separate notebook ready and available during your time of hearing from God. This is reserved exclusively for "other things."

This includes errands, tasks, and duties of any kind—often completely unrelated to what God is talking to you about.

Train Your Eyes to Look at Jesus

*And let us run with perseverance the race marked
out for us, fixing our eyes on Jesus, the pioneer
and perfecter of faith* (Hebrews 12:1-2 NIV).

To receive the pure word of God, it is very important
that your heart be properly focused as you become still. This is
because the intuitive flow comes out of the vision being held
before one's eyes.

If you fix your eyes upon Jesus, the intuitive flow is pure and
comes from Jesus. But if you fix your gaze upon some desire of
your heart, the intuitive flow is affected by that desire. To have

a pure flow you must become still and carefully fix your eyes upon Jesus and Him alone.

Who/what has the object of your attention been during times of prayer and listening to God's voice?

You can trust the flow of spontaneous thoughts when your eyes are fixed upon Jesus. Otherwise, there is a strong likelihood that they are being influenced by other desires or thoughts.

In your time of prayer today, decide to make Jesus your focus. Based on what you have learned so far, engage certain practices that help you do this.

- Singing a worship song
- Overcoming certain distractions of the enemy through key Scripture verses
- Closing your eyes and, based on the visual elements revealed in the Bible, imagining that you are looking upon Christ

Ask the Holy Spirit to show you what strategy to use in fixing your focus upon Jesus. Be sure to write down your experience!

Note: This is not intended to be a formulaic approach to hearing God. However, there are certain practical steps you can take that will help you maintain a consistent focus on Jesus, become still before God, and position yourself to hear Him speak to you.

Remember, *hearing God* is a journey! It is a wonderful adventure and voyage of glorious discovery, and on the other side is the greatest treasure imaginable—a lifestyle where you consistently and clearly hear the Creator of all things speaking directly with you!

Key #3

Fix your eyes upon Jesus and
ask to receive visions.

WATCH AND SEE

I will stand my watch...and watch to see
what He will say to me (Habakkuk 2:1).

HABAKKUK SAID, "I WILL *WATCH TO SEE.*" HABAKKUK WAS actually looking for a vision as he prayed. The Bible is meant to be lived, so decide that you too will begin looking with the eyes of your heart into the spirit world to see what you can see.

This is the biblical inheritance for all believers, as the prophet Joel wrote of our time, saying:

> *And it shall come to pass afterward that I will pour out My Spirit on all flesh; your sons and your daughters shall prophesy, your old men shall dream dreams, your young men shall see visions* (Joel 2:28).

Visions are the inheritance of all Christians, because all Christians are filled with the Holy Spirit. He is the One who gives us eyes to see into the spirit world and receive visions from Heaven.

What do you currently believe/think about receiving visions from God?

_____

_____

_____

Do you believe this is an experience reserved for a "certain kind of Christian"?

_____

_____

_____

How do you feel about the truth that *all* Christians have been given the ability to receive visions (as this is one of the ways that God speaks to His people)?

_____

_____

_____

_____

SET THE LORD
CONTINUALLY BEFORE YOU

I have set the Lord continually before me;
because He is at my right hand, I will
not be shaken (Psalms 16:8 NASB).

TO START EXPERIENCING VISIONS FROM GOD, FOLLOW THE example of King David! This original Psalm makes it clear that it was a decision of David's, not a constant supernatural visitation: "*I have set*" (literally, *I have placed*). This might clear up some of the confusion and mystique concerning visions, as many people believe they are solely the result of ecstatic, otherworldly experiences. While visions are undeniably supernatural and can take on different forms or expressions, one of the key

ways to position yourself to see into spirit world is to make the daily decision to set a clear vision of the Lord ever before your eyes.

Because David knew that the Lord was always with him, he determined in his spirit to see that truth with the eyes of his heart as he went through life, knowing that this would keep his faith strong.

What do you think it means to *set the Lord continually before you*?

_____

_____

_____

Ask the Holy Spirit to give you insight and clarity about this. Then, write down some practical ways that you can *set the Lord before you* in your everyday life.

_____

_____

_____

_____

_____

_____

Hearing

One Picture Is Worth
a Thousand Words

*All these things Jesus spoke to the crowds
in parables, and He did not speak to them
without a parable* (Matthew 13:34 NASB).

WE OFTEN SAY, "A PICTURE IS WORTH A THOUSAND WORDS."

This is certainly true because pictures are the language of
the heart. We notice that Jesus used pictures and images constantly as He taught. God still communicates this way through
the "language" of visions.

When we use pictures in our prayer time, fixing our eyes
on Jesus, we begin speaking the language of the heart and this

moves us quickly into heart/spirit realities getting us beyond our mind.

Take a moment and try to picture the Lord.

Don't go down the standard route here. The end goal is not picturing Jesus like a natural, physical man like we would see in a movie. Instead, ask the Holy Spirit to give you certain images that reveal or embody the character of God as described in Scripture.

What are some specific images that describe and characterize the Lord to you? Write these down and use them during your time listening to God.

_____

_____

_____

_____

_____

_____

_____

_____

_____

Unlock the Power of
Your Godly Imagination

*Because He is at my right hand, I will
not be shaken* (Psalms 16:8 NASB).

Develop a "godly imagination" which *PICTURES THE
things that God says are so.* In Psalm 16, David sets his eyes
to envision a reality that God confirms is truth. In Matthew
28:20, Jesus reminds us, *"I am with you always."* This is a fact to
God, and it should be a fact to us. We need to take what God
considers *facts* and picture them as our reality.

Obviously, if you are picturing that Jesus is *not* with you
that would be picturing a lie, which is unwise. Lies originate
from the "father of lies," and there is no reason for us to be
entertaining these false imaginations or pictures in our minds.

Always see Jesus at your right hand, as David did. Add to this Paul's prayer for God to enlighten the eyes of your heart (see Eph. 1:17-18). Then tune to the flow of the Holy Spirit and watch as He brings the scene alive. You will find that you can step from these godly imaginations into a divine vision.

Take this moment as your opportunity to imagine realities that God says *are so*. This is what develops a godly imagination. Everything we picture and visualize is based on what is revealed as truth in the Scriptures.

You can even start with the truth that David envisions and sets before his mind in Psalms 16:8.

Write down several realities that God says *are so*.

These are the very truths that should provide the foundation for your godly imagination. When our thinking is underscored by the truths that God says *are so*, we are in a safe place to activate the power of godly imagination.

KEEP LOOKING

I kept looking... (Daniel 7:9 NASB).

WE MUST KEEP LOOKING IF WE WANT TO SEE! DANIEL SAW A vision in his mind and said, *"I was looking...I kept looking...I kept looking"* (Dan. 7:2,9,13 NASB).

Perseverance is necessary if we desire to press in to receive visions. Daniel did not give up after one attempt. We need to repent for our tendency to give up so quickly and start presenting the eyes of our hearts to the Lord. Start looking again with the expectation of seeing. Consider the encouraging words of Jesus: *"For everyone who asks receives, and he who seeks finds, and to him who knocks it will be opened"* (Matt. 7:8).

As you pray, look for Jesus. Watch and listen as He speaks to you, revealing and saying the things that are on His heart. Many Christians will find that if they will only look they will see flowing pictures in the same way they receive flowing thoughts.

Why do you think perseverance is so important when it comes to having visions? What are some ways that you can *keep looking* in the place of prayer and listening to God's voice?

A SAMPLE VISION

*"Behold, the virgin shall be with child
and shall bear a Son, and they shall call
His name Immanuel," which translated
means, "God with us"* (Matthew 1:23).

TODAY, I WANT TO GIVE YOU A SAMPLE VISION THAT WILL help activate your godly imagination. Remember, start with truths that God says *are so*.

Jesus Christ is Emmanuel, God with us (see Matt. 1:23). It is as simple as that. You can visualize Christ present with you because *Christ is present with you*. As believers, it is common for us to walk through our lives quoting certain Bible truths but not actually living in their realities. Why? Because we never stop to visualize the reality of that particular truth.

Today, I want you to simply grow quiet before the Lord and consider the powerful reality of *Emmanuel*. This is not simply a name for God that we bring out at Christmastime; this is what the Holy Spirit has brought you into as a child of God. God is with you, for God lives inside of you.

Imagine Christ as forever present with you. He is inside of you. He is with you always.

As you do this, the vision may come so easily that you will be tempted to reject it, thinking that it is just you.

But if you persist in recording these flowing pictures, your doubt will soon be overcome by faith as you recognize that the content of them could only be birthed by Almighty God.

Write down what pictures, images, thoughts, or visions come to your mind as you focus on the reality of *Emmanuel: God with you.*

Note: This is a practice you can start integrating into your everyday walk with God. It will help you see Bible truths as living realities that are not only meant to be studied but lived out.

A LIFESTYLE OF
ABIDING IN CHRIST

Abide in Me, and I in you (John 15:4).

A LIFESTYLE OF CLEARLY HEARING GOD'S VOICE AND SEEING visions is available for every single Christian. It is not reserved for the few special elect; *it is your inheritance.*

Is it possible for you to live out of divine initiative as Jesus did? Yes! It is called *abiding in Christ* (see John 15:4). Fix your eyes upon Jesus. The veil has been torn, giving you access into the immediate presence of God, and He calls you to draw near (see Luke 23:45; Heb. 10:19-22).

The reason many people do not receive visions has nothing to do with God's willingness; it has everything to do with their picture of what *abiding in Christ* looks like. Again, that dividing wall of separation between God and humanity has been torn down the middle. You have been given access to come boldly into God's powerful presence.

Remember, this lifestyle of hearing God is available and much more practical than many of us think. It all begins with getting a clear vision of Jesus by fixing our eyes upon Him, visualizing the truths that God says *are so*, and persevering in the place of expectant, watchful prayer where we *keep looking* for what God wants to show us.

Write down what you envision a lifestyle of abiding in Christ looks like in your life.

Hearing GOD
IN EVERYDAY LIFE

Entering into Godly Imagination through
Journaling and Dialoguing with God

Doug Sterner shares a powerful testimony of how applying this specific key to hearing God's voice brought him into a new level of visions. Review his story and journaling dialogue with God below:

> Once again, I'm excited about the possibility of entering into dialogue with my God and Savior. I really do long to have intimate fellowship—real two-way conversation—with Jesus through the indwelling Holy Spirit. And I really believe it is possible. I believe it because I have experienced it—again!

> *Lord, how would You have me use the eyes of my heart?*

> *Child, dear one, when you picture Me in your mind's eye using your sanctified imagination, you are coming to Me by faith. It's the means I have provided by My Spirit to make our meeting together real to you. It's just a means to an end—a way to consciously be with Me by faith.*

> *You already know in your head that I'm with you, but that's not always enough, is it? You want to feel Me; you want to experience Me. You want to feel My touch and really know Me. By opening the eyes of your heart (something you choose to do), you*

can meet with Me in a very real way that will impact your heart and draw you closer and closer to Me.

So don't hesitate to open your spiritual eyes, the eyes of your imagination, for in so doing you are exercising your faith—without which you cannot please Me. You draw near to Me by faith just as you are saved by faith. Faith sees. Faith pictures. Faith imagines. And when faith is exercised, spiritual reality, My reality, bursts forth. As promised, My Spirit will take over and you will enjoy sweet, precious fellowship with Me that will bless and transform your life and bring Me great delight and joy. I love you, Doug. Come to Me. I'll bless the socks off of you!

In conclusion, I asked:

Lord, how important is journaling in my life?

He responded:

Doug, I know it helps you in your weakness to grab hold of My voice and to record it before it flitters away or you forget. It helps you to capture the bubbling up of My Spirit's thoughts within you. You know, Doug, from your experience today that it can bring great blessing to you because it facilitates relationship and fellowship with Me. It's been real, hasn't it? You have enjoyed meeting with Me today, haven't you? You've been blessed. Journaling facilitated that, and now you have a precious permanent record of our time together. Isn't that encouragement enough to continue?

Key #4

Journaling, the writing out of your prayers and God's answers, brings great freedom in hearing God's voice.

WRITE IT DOWN!

Record the vision and inscribe it on
tablets (Habakkuk 2:2 NASB).

GOD TOLD HABAKKUK TO RECORD THE VISION (SEE HAB. 2:2).
This was not an isolated command. The Scriptures record
many examples of individuals' prayers and God's replies (e.g.
the Psalms, many of the prophets, Revelation). In fact, the Old
Testament placed a high priority on the recorded testimony of
God's words and works. They are memorials, clearly reminding
us of what God said.

This is exactly why *Hearing God* has been presented to
you in this interactive format. The questions and prompts
that fill these pages are not standard. In other words, I do not
expect you to copy them exactly and use them in your future

journaling exercises with God. You are welcome to, especially if the prompts serve as a foundation that you can build upon. Again, what I have given you in this book are simply ways to get you into the habit of asking questions while listening to God and responding to what He speaks back to you. Most likely, the questions that you ask will vary based on what God is saying to you.

Also, journaling helps accurately capture what God is saying to you in a specific moment or season. Our minds are prone to forgetfulness, so when you faithfully write down what God speaks to you, you are preserving the clarity and accuracy of His voice. This is why keeping a written record is so important.

Do you currently journal/keep consistent written record of what God is saying to you?

If not, I encourage you—after you finish going through *Hearing God*, purchase a journal and start to develop a lifestyle of recording your interactions with God.

Convince yourself of the *value* of journaling. We engage as discipline what we perceive as valuable. I want you to take this opportunity to write several reasons *why* you believe it is so important to capture what God is saying to you through keeping a *written record*.

Note: Think about how preserving a written record of what God speaks to you has a powerful impact on your future, on generations to come (your children, grandchildren), on people who are struggling with situations that God has given you victory over, etc.

Write It Down!

WRITE IN THE
FLOW OF FAITH

*He who comes to God must believe that He
is, and that He is a rewarder of those who
diligently seek Him* (Hebrews 11:6).

THIS IS THE PROCESS OF "TWO-WAY JOURNALING," AND I HAVE found it to be a powerful catalyst for clearly discerning God's inner, spontaneous flow. As you journal, you are able to *write in faith* for long periods of time, seamlessly capturing what you believe God is speaking to you. When you are *finished* writing, measure it beside God's written word; the key is making the evaluation upon *completion*. So many of us never step into the divine flow of hearing God's voice because we are, moment

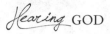

by moment, trying to ascertain whether or not God is actually speaking to us. We are constantly testing what we hear, with the correct intention of trying to avoid deception.

However, testing involves doubt and doubt blocks divine communication, so I do not recommend that you test while you are trying to receive from God (see Heb. 11:6). With journaling, you can receive in faith, knowing that when the flow has ended you can test and examine it carefully, making sure that it lines up with Scripture (see 1 Thess. 5:21).

You might be wondering, *Won't this practice open me up to demonic spirits?* No, because this is not "automatic writing." Before you ever begin the journaling process, pray and completely yield your time of writing to the lordship of Jesus Christ. If Jesus is truly Lord over your life, you are in a safe place.

Come before the Father right now and confess Jesus's lordship over every area of your life. Your mind. Your will. Your emotions. His lordship also includes this time of journaling.

Now, take this time to start writing down what you believe the Holy Spirit is saying to you. Write from the flow of faith in the lined space below. When you are finished, review what you have written and measure it beside the standard of Scripture.

Write in the Flow of Faith

Transformed BY JOURNALING

From Guru to God

This powerful testimony was sent to our ministry from Michael Graham. He started with the following note:

Dear Mark,

In Toronto, 2006, you taught a group of us your journaling technique on "how to hear God's voice." You stated that if we did this consistently for three months it would change our lives. I complied. Indeed I have been journaling in your manner almost daily ever since, and it has been a most comforting, encouraging, and helpful element of my Christian walk. Thank you! Sincerely in Him,

Michael Graham

Here is a sample journal entry from Michael. Note the honesty and authenticity he demonstrates while writing before the Lord. This is why it is so important that we write in that flow of faith, even if we are dealing with difficult and unpleasant topics.

Lord, these days I seem to be making zero progress inside myself as to peace, emotional buoyancy, or lack of flatness or depression! You speak of blessings.

I get none within, though yes, exterior to myself— encouraging circumstances (thank You!) but none inside.

Change my nature! This is my petition. I experience not one single sign of progress—if anything, it's regression. A confession: Your promises seem hollow. They seem always around the corner. My question and statements are being made in earnest. So please respond, Lord.

Now review God's answer to Michael:

Michael, you don't understand the life I give and how My ways work. Do not impatiently expect even measurable changes of temperament and character within yourself. That sort of hope is all "sight," but all My purposes, words, and daily coaching are purposed to build faith in you.

Only faith, actual faith in the face of all circumstances, generates peace. This world and your reactions to it in the absence of faith will always be disquieting. The "quiet" I offer comes through faith in the face of all circumstances. If I was to convert your interior person to one that was—through personality, character or temperament—one unfazed by anything, where would be the need for faith? Can you see now My purpose in allowing your natural self to remain much as it is for the cultivation of necessary faith, the ultimate disposition for any one of My children

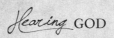

Think, think deeply and regularly on this. You will surely start to get it!

Section Two

MEDITATE ON
GOD'S VOICE

*Meditate within your heart on your
bed, and be still* (Psalms 4:4).

*My eyes anticipate the night watches, that I may
meditate on Your word* (Psalms 119:148 NASB).

MEDITATION

*"God's Spirit utilizing every faculty of my
heart and mind, bringing forth revelation which ushers in transformation."*

Your Next Step in
Hearing God

Once we learn *HOW* God speaks, we need to discover *what* He is saying and revealing to us. Biblical meditation is the key that enables you and I to unlock the mysteries of Heaven in our lives.

Is meditation simply me studying harder?

Is meditation a New Age or eastern technique?

The answer to both questions is *no!*

Meditation is intently seeking God's revelation, resulting in God disclosing Himself to you.

It is the glory of God to conceal a matter. It is the glory of kings to search out a matter (see Prov. 25:2). So we are encouraged to pray for the eyes of our hearts to be enlightened, so we might *know* (see Eph. 1:17-18). God wants you to

hear His voice, yes. But He also wants you to understand and start applying what He is saying to you. Understanding comes through biblical meditation.

HOW TO APPROACH THE MEDITATION PROCESS

This section is broken up into the following segments:

1. *Four Pillars of Biblical Meditation*: Here you will receive a foundation on why meditation is such a necessary part of the Christian life and how it enables us to hear God in greater dimensions. In this section, you will discover *what meditation is* and *why it is beneficial to you.*

2. *Seven-Step Meditation Process*: In this segment, you will learn *how* to practice biblical meditation in seven steps. By the end, you will have an example of what it looks like to go through the process and be able to comfortably model it in your own life.

ENGAGE

This section will be different from the *4 Keys to Hearing God's Voice* as it will not be as directed in the interactive journaling segment.

Why? Now that you have a greater understanding of writing from a flow of faith and journaling, I want you to simply write down what the Holy Spirit speaks to you about each of the Meditation Principles you learn.

In fact, use this opportunity to start practicing and experimenting with these principles. Don't write about how you plan to incorporate them into your daily spiritual disciplines; step out and start to journal about how *you are* meditating on a specific passage of Scripture.

- Write out what Scripture you are talking to God about.

- Reflect on what God is saying back by writing it down.

- Ask the Lord how He wants you to apply a certain Scripture to your everyday life.

Part One

Four Pillars of Biblical Meditation

Pillar #1

MEDITATION IS A CONTINUOUS ACTIVITY

This Book of the Law shall not depart from your mouth, but you shall meditate in it day and night (Joshua 1:8).

WE MEDITATE EVERYWHERE—IN BED, IN THE FIELD, IN THE temple, and while working. We meditate all the time—day, evening, and nighttime. Meditation is our *lifestyle* (see Phil. 4:8). We meditate on God and the things that are of Him— His splendor, His Majesty, His beauty, His Bible, His precepts, His statutes and His ways, His works (i.e. His creation, the world), and His activities (the things He does).

We *don't* meditate on evil, wickedness, or the works of satan.

Describe what meditation as *a continuous activity* looks like to you.

MEDITATION INVOLVES GOD'S SPIRIT UTILIZING EVERY FACULTY OF ONE'S HEART AND MIND

*You shall love the Lord your God with all
your heart, with all your soul, and with
all your mind* (Matthew 22:37).

MEDITATION IS GOD'S SPIRIT IN OUR HEARTS GUIDING EVERY faculty in both hemispheres of our brain. We center down, using quieting music or pulsing, forceful music and/or seeing ourselves present with Him (see Acts 2:25), and we sing, pray, seek, and inquire (including taking our complaints to God to receive His counsel).

We speak, talk, mutter, communicate, babble (probably speaking in tongues), roar (at the enemy and when revelation hits), mourn (repent of our sins), muse, consider, ponder, imagine, study (study is good when wrapped with these other aspects of meditation). We sense the indwelling Holy Spirit crying out for intimacy with the Father (see Gal. 4:6).

Based on this description, consider some of the different expressions of biblical meditation. Have you experienced any of these in your prayer time with God (speak, mutter, speaking in tongues, mourn, roar, muse, etc.)?

Pillar #3

MEDITATION RESULTS IN REVELATION

That the God of our Lord Jesus Christ,
the Father of glory, may give to you a
spirit of wisdom and of revelation in the
knowledge of Him (Ephesians 1:17).

WE QUIET OURSELVES DOWN IN WORSHIP AND PRAYER, ASKING for revelation while fixing our eyes on the Lord who reveals truth to our hearts (see Eph. 1:17-18). We tune to flowing thoughts, visions, emotions, and power from the Holy Spirit within us (see John 7:37-39). We experience our hearts burning with revelations as He opens up the Scriptures to us (see Luke 24:15-32). *His spoken word is powerful* (see Isa. 55:11; John 6:63).

Ask the Holy Spirit to give you a clear view of what revelation is. How would you define revelation, based on what you just read? (A good place to start would be reading Ephesians 1.)

Pillar #4

REVELATION BRINGS TRANSFORMATION!

*But we all, with unveiled face, beholding
as in a mirror the glory of the Lord, are
being transformed into the same image
from glory to glory, just as by the Spirit
of the Lord* (2 Corinthians 3:18).

BURNING REVELATION CREATES LIVING TRUTH IN OUR HEARTS. We say, "Yes, Lord," to these revelations, coming into agreement with what we see Jesus doing and speaking. This results in us being transformed *while we look* at Jesus in action (see 2 Cor. 3:18; 4:17-18).

How do you think revelation takes the Bible and makes it *Living Truth* in your life?

_____

_____

_____

_____

Hearing GOD
IN EVERYDAY LIFE

Transformed by Revelation:
A Reflection on Meditation

One example of revelation bringing transformation was the Lord speaking in my journaling. He said:

> *Mark, whatever you fix your eyes on grows within you, and whatever grows within you, you become.*

Wow! I had been fixing my eyes on my sin, so sin grew within me. Then I fixed my eyes on my efforts to overcome sin through the strength of my flesh, and pride grew within me (or discouragement). Then I fixed my eyes on biblical law and legalism grew within me. Or I fixed my eyes on the anti-Christ and fear grew within me.

Now I fix my eyes on Jesus, and Jesus grows within me! I have experienced lifelong transformation by just this one revelatory word spoken into my heart by the Lord.

These transforming moments can occur continuously if we meditate daily. So we will meditate daily so that we become the radiant expression of Jesus and we make our way prosperous (see 2 Cor. 3:18; 4:18; Heb. 12:2; Josh. 1:8).

Part Two

SEVEN–STEP MEDITATION PROCESS

IN THIS SECTION, I AM GOING TO TAKE YOU STEP BY STEP through the *Seven-step Meditation Process*. This part will be especially interactive, so I encourage you to follow the instructions in order to get the most about of this exercise.

It would be recommended for you to engage one step each day, so you can familiarize yourself with the entire process, little by little. Below, I am giving you a list of all seven steps to the meditation process. This is what we will be studying in the pages ahead.

Breakdown of the Seven-step Meditation Process:

1. Write

2. Quiet Down

3. Reason

4. Speak and Imagine

5. Feel God's Heart

6. Hear God's Rhema

7. Act

Here is how this section will be broken down:

- **Bible Verse:** I recommend that you choose a Scripture verse that you would like to meditate on this week; however, if you would prefer, I will take you through the process using one that I meditated on, Genesis 24:63. This will give you a guided tour of the process.

- **Step:** You will review each step to the meditation process.

- **Dr. Virkler Reflection:** I will share my reflections on Genesis 24:63, giving you a sample of how I have interacted with the meditation process.

- **Journal:** This is where you make it all your own. Write down and record what you say to/hear from the Lord.

How to Meditate on a Topic

1. **Be led by God to the topic:** God will show you the topic He wants you to explore by bringing it to your consciousness through thoughts, the comment of a friend or a book, or a presenting need in your life which demands the revelation and power of God to overcome (see John 16:13).

2. **Be cleansed by His blood:** Approach your meditation time by drawing near to the Lord, repenting of all sins, and asking for and receiving the cleansing of His blood (see Heb. 10:22).

3. **Be humble and teachable:** Ask for the Holy Spirit to reveal truth to you (see Eph. 1:17-18). Be willing to discover and embrace His truth, no matter

what it costs (reputation, pride, ego, job, financial security, etc.).

4. **Be fearless:** Some churches will excommunicate, fire, or shun a person who disagrees with the church's belief. Thus fear hinders many from pursuing truth. Put your whole trust in God to sustain you, even if you are shunned or rejected by organized religion.

5. **Be wholehearted in your search:** Seek the Lord with your whole heart (i.e. presenting all your faculties to the Lord to fill and to use) and you will find Him (see Jer. 29:13). Ask the Holy Spirit to guide and fill your heart and then tune to flowing thoughts, flowing pictures, flowing emotions.

6. **Let the Holy Spirit guide you in the use of the following Bible tools:**

   - A good concordance such as *Strong's Exhaustive Concordance* and the *King James Concordance* (gives you every verse where a specific Hebrew or Greek word is used).

   - Some good Bible dictionaries such as *Strong's Hebrew and Greek Dictionaries, Brown-Driver-Briggs Dictionary, Vines Complete Bible Dictionary of New Testament Words, Vines Complete Dictionary of Old Testament Words.*

   - Miscellaneous analytical tools such as *Nave's Topical Bible* and *Manners and Customs of the Bible*, etc.

- Interpretive tools such as exegetical commentaries, expository commentaries, and devotional commentaries.

7. **Receive counsel:** Wisdom and safety come from receiving counsel, input, and confirmation from the five-fold team God has given to you (see Prov. 11:14; Eph. 4:11; 2 Cor. 13:1).

Step One

WRITE

Record the vision and inscribe it on tablets (Habakkuk 2:2 NASB).

COPY THE VERSE BY HAND ONTO A PIECE OF PAPER OR THREE by five card and keep it with you to meditate on, memorize, and mutter throughout the day. Also, record the verse in the lined space below (see Deut. 17:18).

By the time you are finished with this guided exercise, going through the seven-step process, the goal is for you to have your own meditation journal. There, you can record Scriptures and the revelation you receive while meditating on those passages.

Choose a Bible verse that you would like to meditate on.

REFLECTION FROM DR. VIRKLER

If you do not have one, you can start with Genesis 24:63 and I will help guide you through the meditation process.

And Isaac went out to meditate in the field in the evening; and he lifted his eyes and looked, and there, the camels were coming.

JOURNAL

Write down the Scripture verse you choose for the meditation exercise.

Step Two

QUIET DOWN

*Surely I have composed and quieted
my soul* (Psalms 131:2 NASB).

BECOME STILL IN GOD'S PRESENCE, LOVING HIM THROUGH
soft soaking/quiet worship music (see 2 Kings 3:15-16) and/or
praying in tongues (see 1 Cor. 14:14). *Imagine* that Jesus is with
you during this process. The Holy Spirit is inside you, desiring
to take truth and turn it into revelation. Tune in to His flowing
thoughts, pictures, and emotions (see John 7:37-39).

Do *not* journal until after you have engaged this process.
Then you can reflect on the journey through writing. Right
now, the key is learning how to quiet yourself down in God's
presence and position yourself to meditate on what He is saying
to you.

REFLECTION FROM DR. VIRKLER

With this verse, I used the Sea of Galilee Quieting Exercise, picturing myself together with Jesus and tuned to flow.
This exercise is available for free at www.cwgministries.org/
galilee.

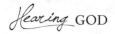

JOURNAL

How did the process of quieting down go for you today? Describe your journey below.

Step Three

REASON

"Come now, and let us reason together,"
says the Lord (Isaiah 1:18).

NOW, YOU WILL REASON TOGETHER WITH GOD ABOUT THE
Scripture. This means that the Holy Spirit will guide your reasoning process (i.e. through flow).

Ask questions like: "Lord, what do You want to show me
about any of the following?"

- the context of a verse
- the Hebrew/Greek definitions of the key words
  in the verse
- any cultural understandings

REFLECTION FROM DR. VIRKLER

Based on the Scripture example, Genesis 24:63, here is a
glimpse into my time of reasoning with the Lord. This is what
He spoke to my heart during the process:

> *Meditation is a lifestyle that I have ordained. Do it in*
> *the evening. It is better than watching television. As*
> *you do it, I can and will bring the choicest provisions*

of life to you. In this case, Isaac lifted up his eyes and saw the gift of his future wife who was being brought to him by his servant. His servant had discovered her in a distant land through a divine appointment. I also bring good gifts to you from distant places while you honor Me by making meditation your lifestyle. For when you honor Me by inviting Me into your everyday life, I honor you by bringing to you divine appointments. Honor Me with your lifestyle. Let your lifestyle be one of ongoing meditation.

JOURNAL

Write out what the Lord shares with you as you reason through your Scripture verse together with Him.

Be sure to ask Him the questions that are presented above.

Step Four

SPEAK AND IMAGINE

PONDER THE SCRIPTURE, SPEAKING IT TO YOURSELF SOFTLY over and over again until you can say it with your eyes closed.

As you repeat the Scripture, allow yourself to see it with the eyes of your heart. Note what the picture is in your mind's eye as you repeat the Scripture.

REFLECTION FROM DR. VIRKLER

Based on the Scripture example, Genesis 24:63, this is what I see:

> *I see Isaac walking in a field in the evening and pondering as he walks along. I see Jesus at his side, speaking with him.*

JOURNAL

Write down the pictures that come to your mind as you repeat the Scripture verse to yourself and start to see it with the eyes of your heart.

Step Five

FEEL GOD'S HEART

WHILE IMAGINING THE SCRIPTURE (AS OUTLINED IN STEP four), ask: "Lord, what does this Scripture reveal about Your heart toward me?" Feel His heart and journal it out.

REFLECTION FROM DR. VIRKLER

Based on the Scripture example, Genesis 24:63, this is what I feel is God's heart toward me:

> *Mark, I love to walk with you in the cool of the day. This was My original design. This allows you to hear My thoughts and receive My wisdom, My counsel, and My blessing. It is My desire to love you and care for you and provide for you and this is one key way I can do that if you allow Me to. Come experience My heart toward you in the cool of the day. Come meditate in the cool of the day.*

JOURNAL

Write down what you feel God's heart *toward* you is through your verse.

Step Six

HEAR GOD'S *RHEMA*

*For the word of God is living and
active and sharper than any two-edged
sword* (Hebrews 4:12 NASB).

PUT YOURSELF IN THE PICTURE OF THIS SCRIPTURE IN YOUR mind.

Ask, "Lord, what are You speaking to me through this Scripture?" Tune to the flowing thoughts and flowing pictures (God's voice and vision) and record this dialogue in your two-way journaling.

REFLECTION FROM DR. VIRKLER

Based on the Scripture example, Genesis 24:63, this is what I believe that God is actively speaking to me:

> *Mark, there is so much I want to reveal to you, and I do it as we take these walks together in the cool of the day. You see, this was My pattern in the Garden of Eden. I chose for it to be our pattern also, that we walk together down the road of life. Will you come to Me in the cool of the day and meditate in My presence, allowing Me to minister grace to you on*

a daily basis? You can ponder the specific needs and situations you are surrounded by and present them to Me, and I will give you revelation and insight as to how to best handle them and respond to them. I will do this daily if you will walk with Me daily. You will experience ideas and understanding beyond your natural ability. You will accomplish beyond your natural giftings.

JOURNAL

Write down and record what the Lord is actively speaking to you about your Scripture verse.

Step Seven

ACT

*Blessed are those who hear the word of God
and observe it (Luke 11:28 NASB).*

ACCEPT THE REVELATION GOD IS SPEAKING TO YOU AND repent of any sin that is opposite of it. Repentance is two-fold. While it involves experiencing godly sorrow over our sin, it also transforms the way we think. The Holy Spirit is inviting you to adjust the way you think—and ultimately the way you live—to come into alignment with His revelation.

Speak it forth and then act on it! Meditation is all about producing a lifestyle where we start living out the Word of God.

REFLECTION FROM DR. VIRKLER

Here is an example of what I have prayed back to the Lord in response to His revelation:

Lord, I accept this awesome invitation from You, my Lord and my Redeemer. What a gracious gift You have offered me, and all I have to do is say yes and we walk together. I receive Your life and fullness into my heart and life. Lord, what an amazing offer You are making.

I roar at every false belief that I can do it on my own. That is a lie from satan; I renounce humanism and rationalism. Get out of my life, now! I choose to die daily and come alive only to Jesus, who is my life.

Lord, I will walk with You and talk with You in the cool of the day, and I will present to You the issues I am facing and ask for Your wisdom and insight on them. I thank You, Lord, for Your gracious wisdom, revelation, and strength which flow so freely!

JOURNAL

Write down your response to God's revelation in the form of an *action prayer*.

Ask the Lord how He wants you to integrate this meditation into your everyday life and then purpose in your spirit to do it.

Hearing GOD
IN EVERYDAY LIFE

Releasing God's Healing Power through the Seven-step Healing Model

One practical way that we can act on hearing God's voice is through the ministry of healing. This is not reserved for a special type of Christian; all believers have received the power of the Holy Spirit and have been commissioned to heal the sick.

Also, all believers are able to flow in the gifts of the Holy Spirit. As you develop a lifestyle of hearing God's voice, expect Him to speak to you—clearly and specifically—about people He wants to touch with His healing power.

When you come in contact with these individuals, here is a simple seven-step model for you to follow as you pray for their healing and watch God perform the miraculous in their lives.

1. *Express Compassion.* Smile, ask their name, express love to them, "Of course Jesus wants to heal you...Jesus includes everyone...you absolutely are included."

2. *Ask.* "What's Wrong?" "Where does it hurt?" and then, "May I pray for you?" Focus intently on *one* item at a time.

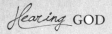

3. *Become Still and Listen to God.* Ask, "How should I pray for this person?" Relax, smile, and receive, tuning to flowing thoughts and flowing pictures as your eyes are fixed on Jesus. If no special revelation bubbles up, then minister healing based on the promises in the Bible and Jesus's example of healing *all*. Maybe ask the person, "How long have you had this and what event occurred at the time this problem began?" To receive words of knowledge, you should *ask for them,* receiving any "miscellaneous" information the Lord may want to reveal through the above means while also tuning to spontaneous emotions, spontaneous bodily sensations, and spontaneous pictures/words of body parts. Step out in faith and lovingly share them.

4. *Invite God's Presence, His Compassion, and Power to Heal.* "Lord, pour *Your love* and healing power on this person. Holy Spirit, we welcome Your presence." With your eyes open, watch the person for signs of the Holy Spirit moving upon them (eyelids flutter, become flushed, gentle trembling, peace). *Now*, the love and power of the Lord is present to heal! (See Luke 5:17.)

5. *Command the Healing in Jesus's Name.* Lay your hand on the infirm spot (be sensitive when praying for opposite sex). Command the affliction/pain to leave. Use short prayers (ten to twenty seconds). Both client and prayer counselor are

to stay relaxed and smiling so you do not block the flow of the Holy Spirit. Maintain this attitude: "Healing is easy because Jesus has already done the work." (See Isaiah 53:4-5; Psalms 103:3; 147:3.) *"Because Jesus is alive, tonight the blind will see, the lame will walk, the deaf will hear."* Rebuke demons and command pain to go. Speak restoration and normal function of all cells and body parts. "Function normally in Jesus's name!" See God's light penetrating the area. You focus God's healing light on the infirm spot just as you would focus a magnifying glass on a piece of paper so that the sun's rays are intensified and start it on fire. God's focused healing power releases miracles (see Luke 11:34-36; Hab. 3:4). You are simply declaring, believing and seeing His divine energy penetrate the area.

6. *Test It Out.* Invite them to thank God for the healing as they do something they could not easily do before. Miracles manifest *as they step out in faith,* believing, *thanking,* and *receiving* in childlike joy (see Mark 11:22-24). As the lepers *went,* they were healed (see Luke 17:14). "Get up and walk."

7. *Repeat.* Pray a second, third, and fourth time. If you pray and you see no visible change or you see a partial healing, then pray again (immediately) until you have prayed three to four times

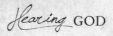

and either they are completely healed or you note no further improvement (see Matt. 7:7-8; Luke 18:1-8; Mark 8:23-25). These prayers do not need to be any longer than your initial prayer. Close by praying a blessing. Finally, be sure to determine if they have ever invited Christ into their lives. If not, lead them in a simple salvation prayer.

Hearing GOD
IN EVERYDAY LIFE

Success with the Seven-step Meditation Process

I used this technique and it was one of the most intimate times I have had with the Lord in quite a while. Bottom line: I found this seven-step process very effective and I plan to use it more in the future. Below is a sample journal entry as I used this method.

—PASTOR JIM FRENCH

"Do not let your heart be troubled; believe in God, believe also in Me" (John 14:1 NASB).

As I meditated on this verse, the Lord showed me a vision of a heart—my heart which was pierced with arrows. I asked Him what the arrows were and what He wanted to tell me.

MY JOURNAL ENTRY

This is what I believe the Lord spoke to me:

Son, our hearts are fused—they are one. But there are some aspects of your heart that you have not completely yielded to me. I await your decision to do so.

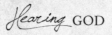

The arrows you saw were wounds in your heart from people and events—past hurts and pains. The choice is yours to hold on to them or release them. But if you choose to deal with the wounds yourself, the arrows will remain. Only I can truly remove the arrows and heal the wounds, but you must yield these to me.

Jim, the ministry places you in a position of vulnerability. I ask you to pour your life into people who may not accept you as My servant and messenger. They too have their own pain which will not allow them to trust. In ministering, you must not allow rejection to penetrate your heart.

Remember, you were not sent to heal—I was. Your job is to present Me in every situation, and any acceptance or rejection is acceptance or rejection of Me. You must make a conscious decision to not accept any rejection or you will be wounded again. The wounds in your heart make it more difficult for Me to minister through you. Yield these wounds and the people who inflicted them to Me, and I will heal you.

Here is my response:

Yes, Lord. I release these wounds and the people who inflicted them to You. Forgive me for hanging on to them. I repent and ask for Your grace to not allow hurt to penetrate my heart again. Thank You, Lord!

MEDITATION JOURNAL

ONCE YOU HAVE FINISHED GOING THROUGH THIS SECTION, I would encourage you to purchase a separate journal for biblical meditation. Here, you will be able to write down different Scriptures and take them through the entire process.

For now, I would like to provide you with several pages where you can begin engaging this process in your everyday life.

Step 1: Write

_____

_____

_____

Step 2: Quiet Down

_____

_____

Step 3: Reason

Step 4: Speak and Imagine

Step 5: Feel God's Heart

Step 6: Hear God's Rhema

Step 7: Act

Section Three

HEARING GOD THROUGH YOUR DREAMS

*I will bless the Lord who has counseled
me; indeed, my mind instructs me in
the night* (Psalms 16:7 NASB).

*Your young men shall see visions, your old
men shall dream dreams* (Acts 2:17).

WHY ARE DREAMS IMPORTANT TO US TODAY?

GOD HAS CHOSEN TO SPEAK WITH HUMANKIND THROUGH dreams. He guides and counsels us through our dreams. He establishes covenants with us through our dreams. He grants us gifts in our dreams. Scripture shows us that God has utilized dreams from Genesis to Revelation, and it also reveals that He would continue to use them in the last days. As you get ready to conclude this introductory journey into hearing God, I invite you to reconsider the amount of importance you place on your dream life.

Remember, God is always speaking. He is constantly communicating with His people. We must position ourselves in a place where we are able to clearly and consistently hear His voice. This is why we began by reviewing the *4 Keys to Hearing*

God's Voice. These are absolutely foundational if we want to live a life of confidently hearing from Heaven.

We took it to the next level by studying biblical meditation, particularly the *Seven-step Process to Biblical Meditation*. Once we hear from God, we are given a responsibility for what He said to us. Whether we hear from the voice of the Holy Spirit speaking directly to us or hear Him speaking to us through the pages of Scripture, our responsibility is the same—*action*. We must be good stewards of God's voice.

Meditation is a powerful tool that helps us internalize what God is saying so that we can become well-equipped to live it out in our everyday lives. Meditation is truly a catalyst to lifestyle transformation. Some hear God's voice but never do anything with what He says. However, by pursuing a lifestyle of biblical meditation, we are saying back to God, "I want to be one who hears *from* You, and I want to be transformed by what I hear." The person who lives this way positions him/herself to consistently hear God's voice. God is looking for good and faithful stewards who put His Word to work in their lives.

BECOME A STEWARD OF GOD'S DREAM MESSAGES

God is calling His people to reexamine the night hours. Consider that when you total up all dreams and visions in the Bible and all the stories and actions which come out of these dreams and visions, you have about one-third of the Bible. This is equal to the size of the New Testament! This reveals that dreams are a central way God has chosen to communicate with us, and thus they *must* be given great weight. We must learn how to steward what God speaks to us in the night. In the final pages of our journey together, I want to help you begin this process in your life.

The Bible declares that God counsels us at night through our dreams (see Ps. 16:7), and it is full of examples and illustrations of this principle. In the dreams recorded throughout Scripture, God gives wise direction concerning the next steps for people to take. He grants wisdom and encourages people in faith. He shows them how to escape coming calamity and how to provide for their families in the midst of imminent disasters. God even enters into covenants with people and grants them gifts in their dreams! These examples reinforce the truth that our dream lives are significant.

As you interact with the pages ahead, you will start learning how to explore your own dreams. The most important application to take away from this section is simply *your dreams are important and should be recorded.* This is the discipline I would like to help you start including in your life.

In the same way you are learning to journal and meditate, I want you to routinely record the dreams that you dream. Start bringing them before the Lord and ask Him for wisdom, clarity, and interpretation.

All of us can learn to hear from God during the two hours of dream life that we have each night. This final section is designed to give you some basic tools on how to identify and start learning to interpret the dreams God gives you.

In addition, the corresponding journal pages will help you develop a regular habit of recording what God is saying to you through your dreams.

Seven Reasons We Should Listen to Our Dreams

Before you start writing down and recording your dreams, it is important that you understand *why* dreams are so important to begin with.

Reflect on the following seven reasons why you should listen to your dreams.

1. God declared that He *would* speak through dreams and visions in the Old Testament.

    Then He said, "Hear now My words: If there is a prophet among you, I, the Lord, make Myself known to him in a vision; I speak to him in a dream" (Numbers 12:6).

2. God declared that He *did* speak through dreams and visions in the Old Testament.

    I have also spoken by the prophets, and have multiplied visions; I have given symbols through the witness of the prophets (Hosea 12:10).

3. God declares that He *will* communicate through dreams and visions in the New Testament.

    "And it shall be in the last days," God says, "that I will pour forth of My Spirit on all mankind; and your sons and your daughters shall prophesy, and your young men shall see visions, and your old men shall dream dreams" (Acts 2:17 NASB).

4. God declares that He *will counsel* us at night through our dreams.

    I will bless the Lord who has given me counsel; my heart also instructs me in the night seasons (Psalms 16:7).

5. Rather than our dreams being fatalistic, dreams are calling us to change *so we will not perish.*

    Indeed God speaks once, or twice, yet no one notices it. In a dream, a vision of the night, when sound sleep falls on men, while they slumber in their beds, then He opens the ears of men, and seals their instruction, that He may turn man aside from his conduct, and keep man from pride; He keeps back his soul from the pit, and his life from passing over into Sheol (Job 33:14-18 NASB).

6. God does very significant things *within* dreams. For example, He established the Abrahamic Covenant in a dream.

   Now when the sun was going down, a deep sleep fell upon Abram; and behold, terror and great darkness fell upon him. God said to Abram, "Know for certain that your descendants will be strangers in a land that is not theirs, where they will be enslaved and oppressed four hundred years." ...On that day the Lord made a covenant with Abram, saying, "To your descendants I have given this land, from the river of Egypt as far as the great river, the river Euphrates" (Genesis 15:12-13,18 NASB).

7. God grants supernatural gifts *through* dreams.

   In Gibeon the Lord appeared to Solomon in a dream at night; and God said, "Ask what you wish Me to give you."

   "...So give Your servant an understanding heart to judge Your people to discern between good and evil. For who is able to judge this great people of Yours?"

   "...Behold, I have done according to your words. Behold, I have given you a wise and discerning heart, so that there has been no one like you before you, nor shall one like you arise after you."

   ...Then Solomon awoke, and behold, it was a dream. And he came to Jerusalem and stood before the ark of the covenant of the Lord, and offered burnt offerings and made peace offerings, and made a feast for all his servants (1 Kings 3:5,9,12,15 NASB).

Dream Dedication

Take this opportunity to write a personal prayer of dedication to the Lord as you begin to explore this subject.

- Ask Him to lead and direct you.
- Invite the Holy Spirit to bring clarity.
- Above all, pray that your ability to hear God's voice through your dreams would increase.

Now, start dedicating your times of rest to the Lord. Before you go to sleep tonight, ask Him to speak to you through your dreams.

Also, ask the Holy Spirit to help you clearly remember your dreams so you can write them down.

YOUR SEVEN-DAY
DREAM JOURNAL

FOR THE NEXT *SEVEN DAYS*, WRITE DOWN YOUR DREAMS ON the following pages. Record them in as much detail as you can. *Do not try to interpret them.* If you sense the Lord is giving you clarity on a particular dream or something uniquely stands out to you, write it down elsewhere and refer to it once you receive more instruction in dream interpretation.

For now, simply write down what you remember dreaming and keep this information in this journal. You will have seven days' worth of lined space available. If you cannot remember your dream, simply write, "Did not remember."

After you finish writing out your dreams, I have included a few testimonies of how God has spoken to individuals through their dreams. Read their firsthand accounts and discover the life-changing impact that your dreams have.

Before you start, here are *five practical things you can do to help recall your dreams*:

1. *Say* to yourself, "I believe dreams contain a valid message."

   This is a signal to your heart that you are taking the process seriously and want to hear what God wants to speak to you through your dreams. You are giving your heart permission, and even asking it to awaken you after each dream. Your heart will do exactly that. If you do not awaken within five minutes of the dream ending, you will not recall it. If, however, you tell your heart that dreams are nothing more than leftover undigested pizza, then your heart lets you sleep through the dream and does not awaken you after it is over. As a result, you do not recall it.

2. *Ask* God to speak to you through dreams as you fall asleep.

   God does answer prayers, especially when they are prayed in accordance with His will!

3. *Put* this journal beside your bed and immediately record your dreams upon awakening.

   You will forget most of your dreams by the morning, so be sure to get up and write them down when you awaken.

4. *Get* eight hours of sleep, as the entire last hour will be dream-time.

5. *Awaken* naturally, without the use of an alarm clock.

   Alarms actually shatter dream recall and blast tidbits of dreams into oblivion where they are never found.

Day One

MY DREAM

Hearing GOD
IN EVERYDAY LIFE

A Wake-up Shaking

I love hearing testimonies of God speaking to His children through their dreams and night visions. And Elizabeth Kiessling's story is one awesome example! I'll let her share the powerful experience in her own words.

> I had a very encouraging dream about my son, one that really set me free. My son was 19 and was not really pursuing the Lord ardently. He received Jesus young and even spoke in tongues but seemed to cool off in his teens and as he went to college.
>
> We had numerous bad trials that really rocked us, and perhaps him as well. I don't know. Our hearts have been toward him and we continued to pray for Jesus to encounter him, touch his heart, and wake him up again. He had friends who were not following the Lord, drinking and smoking weed, partying every weekend.
>
> So, here is the exciting part.
>
> One night I had a dream. I saw a long dining table, my daughter was sitting there talking to another young lady, and my son was at the other end with his head down on his arms asleep.

All of a sudden Jesus came in. I saw Him; He was dressed in a long beautiful blue tunic with pants underneath. Gold embroidery surrounded the sleeves and the front up around his neck. He had a very large beautiful crown on His head. He walked up to my son, bent over, and began to gently shake his arm as if to wake him up!

Hallelujah! Yahoo! Praise the Lamb! I just thank Him every day for encouraging me where my son is concerned and know that Jesus has this taken care of. I don't worry anymore—yay God!

May this encourage all parents with wayward children.

Elizabeth Kiessling

Day Two

MY DREAM

_____

_____

_____

_____

_____

_____

_____

_____

_____

_____

_____

_____

_____

_____

_____

Day Three

MY DREAM

_____

_____

_____

_____

_____

_____

_____

_____

_____

_____

_____

_____

_____

_____

Hearing GOD
IN EVERYDAY LIFE

Counsel to Not Purchase a House

The following story from Don Swartzlander shows how God will give us very practical instruction through our dreams.

> God called our family of six to leave our home, relatives, and job in Pennsylvania and go to Bible college in New York State. He gave us that "word" in late July. We were thinking that "someday" we would go, but we were told by our pastor that we could be in school that September. So we left our five-, four-, three-, and one-year-olds with relatives for a three-day weekend and went to Lima, New York to look for a job and housing.
>
> We spent every daylight hour looking for places to live and work. It was frustrating searching with no success and time was running out. Most places were either too small, too expensive, or too far from the school.
>
> My wife and I looked at one house that was about ten miles away, and it seemed like it would meet our needs. However, we would have to make the decision whether to buy it or not in the next 24 hours. We thought that it was the only one that would fit,

so maybe it was an example of how "God was sup-plying." Sue and I prayed and went to bed in the guest wing of the school.

In my sleep, I had a dream. In the dream I was in jail. I was holding onto and looking out through heavy steel bars. But the funny thing about the jail was that I knew the door was closed, but not locked. I could get myself out. All I had to do was open the door and walk out. But I was still inside looking out.

In the morning I told my wife about the dream. I asked her what she thought, and she suggested we ask God about it. We did, and He told me that it was up to me/us if we bought the house or not. But if we did buy it, we would be "locked up" by that purchase and really not be free to do what He wanted us to. It was our/my decision to be bound or be free.

We decided to "be free" and not to buy the house. That meant we were free, but we had less than twelve hours left to find a place to live. We went into the lounge and sat on a couch wondering what to do next. Being summer, there were not many people on campus. One of the maintenance workers (a grad-uated student) came down the hall. He introduced himself and asked us what we were doing there. We told him. He said that he rarely went that way but God had directed him there for some unknown rea-son. Now he knew why. He went on to say that he

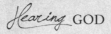

and his family had graduated and were moving on into ministry. The four bedroom house they lived in might be available when they moved that week.

We tried to contact the landlord, but his wife said he was golfing. We had to leave for home so we got directions to the golf course. Once there I hopped in a golf cart and hunted for her husband. I found him and he was puzzled why someone would be searching for him. He asked, "What do you want?" I told him we would like to rent his house. He reached out and shook my hand. He said my handshake was good enough for him and he rented us the house right there on the golf course.

We lived in that house for the next four years. Praise God for the protection, freedom, and guidance He provided in *a dream*.

Day Four

MY DREAM

_____

_____

_____

_____

_____

_____

_____

_____

_____

_____

_____

_____

_____

_____

_____

Hearing

MY DREAM

 Hearing GOD
IN EVERYDAY LIFE

The King's Dancers Christian School of Performing Arts and Worship: Birthed out of Hearing God's Voice and Dreaming His Dreams

Suzanne Cerniglia shares her incredible story about how God used a dream to birth a school that is leading multitudes into new artistic expressions of worship and creativity.

My name is Suzanne Cerniglia and I am the founder and co-owner of the King's Dancers Christian School of Performing Arts located in Schenectady, New York. I would like to tell you a little about my testimony of how the school came about.

In 2002, I had recently gotten married to my husband Salvatore Cerniglia at a young age of 19 years. I had completed a two-year degree in early childhood education in a community college just before getting married. I really felt in my heart that there was something special for me to do as a career, so I began to pray for God's perfect will for my life.

Around this time my husband, Salvatore, introduced me to Mark Virkler's courses at Christian Leadership University—specifically "Communion with God" and "Wisdom through Dream

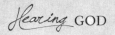

Interpretation." It was while I was taking these classes that God revealed to me His special calling for my life.

While I was taking the classes I decided to enroll in nursing school. I felt like I would be a good pediatric nurse, so I completed the first year and was starting my second year when just then I had my first dream in the night regarding my calling.

Dream One: In my dream I was on a hospital floor and all my other classmates where in their nursing uniforms. However, I was the only one not in my uniform, but was actually in a classical ballet leotard and tutu. I felt so out of place in my dream. I did not think much about that dream, but I did write it down in my dream journal.

I continued with my nursing school at that point and about one month later received another significant dream.

Dream Two: Down from Heaven was sent a very colorful dancing streamer. I jumped up and grabbed it and started climbing up the streamer into Heaven. There I found that I was standing in front of the Living God! He spoke to me in a low and beautiful voice. He said, "Now you are ready." Just then He proceeded to pour what looked like gold paint from the top of my head all the way down my body until I was covered with gold paint. Then I awoke. I immediately wrote down all I could remember in that dream in my dream journal. It was so powerful, but I still did not know what I was ready for.

Then came Dream Three. It was very clear and outright for me to know what God wanted in my life. The Lord said in my ear in an audible voice, "Go look in your journal." At this same time I was keeping a journal as part of the "Communion with God" course which teaches you how to hear God's voice. I began to walk to my journal in the dream and opened it up. The words were large and black and they said "Christian Dance Studio 2002."

God could not have spoken any clearer to me than in this dream. I do feel that through understanding dream interpretation and especially writing down these significant dreams, God revealed the plan He had for my life. I feel fulfilled, and I know without a doubt that God has made me to bring Him glory by teaching others to dance for His glory.

The King's Dancers has grown considerably since starting with four students in the basement of my sister-in-law's house. The King's Dancers now has over 165 students ages 4 to adult, a staff of 9 teachers, and are in 4 locations within a 60-mile radius. We offer a variety of types of dance and worship including ballet, tap, Irish step, hip-hop, flag and banner technique, and incorporating into prophetic drama.

What is amazing is that we do very little marketing for the dance school. It is so clear that God is

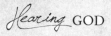

behind what we are doing, because He just sends the students and teachers effortlessly. Praise be to our God! Since 2002 the King's Dancers have been able to perform at Christian events, secular high schools, special church services, and other events in our local community. We have been featured by our local newspaper, the *Albany Times Union*, which did an extensive article and video on the King's Dancers. We did not seek them out—the *Albany Times Union* sought us out for unknown reasons. They were so intrigued with and interested in our Christian dance school.

What is truly amazing and scriptural is how one or two dreams and one or two journals can change your whole life's direction and destiny. I love God more than ever and love my vocation and ministry. There is no other way all this could have happened if it was not for Him! If you connect to Him, you will connect with your destiny!

Day Six

MY DREAM

Hearing

_____

_____

_____

_____

_____

_____

_____

_____

_____

_____

_____

_____

_____

_____

MY DREAM

_____

_____

_____

_____

_____

_____

_____

_____

_____

_____

_____

_____

_____

_____

Seven Foundational Principles for Dream Interpretation

1. Most dreams are symbolic (including biblical dreams), so view them the same way you would view a political cartoon.

   Throw the switch in your brain that says, "Look at this symbolically." You can learn the art of communicating symbolically by playing the game Pictionary or Bible Pictionary.

2. The symbols will come from the dreamer's life, so ask, "What does this symbol mean to me?" or, if you working on another's dream, ask, "What does this symbol mean to you?"

   For example, Joseph was a shepherd, and he

dreamed of sheaves and the sun, moon, and stars bowing down (see Gen. 37:1-11). These images surround a shepherd boy who lives in the fields.

Nebuchadnezzar, a king, dreamed of statues of gold (see Dan 2:31), which surround kings who live in palaces.

3. The dream generally speaks of the concerns which your heart is currently facing. So ask, "What issues was I processing the day before I had the dream?"

    For example, Paul was wondering where to go next on his missionary journey and had a dream of a Macedonian man motioning for him to come on over (see Acts 16:6-11).

    Nebuchadnezzar was thinking his kingdom would go on forever (see Dan. 4:28-33) and he had a dream of a tree being chopped off at the roots (see Dan. 4:9-27). Once you know the thoughts that were on the dreamer's heart when he fell asleep, it is much easier to draw out the meaning of the dream.

4. The meaning of the dream must be drawn from the dreamer.

    Realize you know nothing about the dream, but through dependence upon the Holy Spirit and the skillful use of questions you can draw the meaning of the dream out from the heart of the dreamer.

    As for these four young men, God gave them knowledge and skill in all literature and wisdom;

and Daniel had understanding in all visions and dreams (Daniel 1:17).

A plan in the heart of a man is like deep water, but a man of understanding draws it out (Proverbs 20:5 NASB).

5. The dreamer's heart will leap and "witness" and say, "Aha!" when it hears the right interpretation, so never accept an interpretation that does not bear witness in the dreamer's heart.

6. Dreams reveal but do not condemn.

   Their goal is to preserve life, not to destroy it (see Job 33:13-18).

7. Never make a major decision in your life based only on a dream without receiving additional confirmation from the other ways that God speaks to us and guides us (peace in our hearts, the counsel of others, illumined Scriptures, God's still small voice, prophecy, anointed reasoning, etc.).

Revisit Your Seven-day Dream Journal

Go back to your seven days of recorded dreams. Begin to work through each dream using the following seven principles for dream interpretation. These are extremely basic and foundational. They will take you to a certain level, but we strongly encourage you to seek out other resources for a more detailed and exhaustive approach to dream interpretation.

Remember, this is simply an introduction to hearing God through your dreams. The goal here is not necessarily interpretation; rather, it is to get you into a habit of constantly paying attention to the dreams you have and understand that God is speaking to you through your dreams.

For this section, I encourage you to take each dream through the seven-step process in the pages ahead.

DREAM FROM DAY ONE

1. Identify symbols in your dream (remember to see it from a symbolic perspective).

_____

_____

2. Because the symbols come from your life, ask yourself, "What does this symbol mean to me?"

_____

_____

3. Ask yourself, "What issue was I processing the day before I had the dream?" Write it down.

_____

_____

4. Ask the Holy Spirit to help you understand the meaning of your dream. Write down some ideas of what you think the dream *might* mean.

5. Identify how your heart bears witness to the different interpretation options.

6. What do you believe the dream is revealing? (Remember, dreams reveal; they don't condemn.)

7. Seek additional confirmation. If you believe you have received clarity on a dream, be sure to submit to several sources for review/evaluation first between acting upon it. Remember, never make a major decision in your life based only on a dream without receiving additional confirmation from the other ways that God speaks to us and guides us (peace in our hearts, the counsel of others, illumined Scriptures, God's still small voice, prophecy, anointed reasoning, etc.).

Hearing

Dream from Day Two

1. Identify symbols in your dream (remember to see it from a symbolic perspective).

_____

_____

2. Because the symbols come from your life, ask yourself, "What does this symbol mean to me?"

_____

_____

3. Ask yourself, "What issue was I processing the day before I had the dream?" Write it down.

_____

_____

4. Ask the Holy Spirit to help you understand the meaning of your dream. Write down some ideas of what you think the dream *might* mean.

5. Identify how your heart bears witness to the different interpretation options.

6. What do you believe the dream is revealing? (Remember, dreams reveal; they don't condemn.)

7. Seek additional confirmation. If you believe you have received clarity on a dream, be sure to submit to several sources for review/evaluation first between acting upon it. Remember, never make a major decision in your life based only on a dream without receiving additional confirmation from the other ways that God speaks to us and guides us (peace in our hearts, the counsel of others, illumined Scriptures, God's still small voice, prophecy, anointed reasoning, etc.).

Hearing

DREAM FROM DAY THREE

1. Identify symbols in your dream (remember to see it from a symbolic perspective).

   _____

   _____

2. Because the symbols come from your life, ask yourself, "What does this symbol mean to me?"

   _____

   _____

3. Ask yourself, "What issue was I processing the day before I had the dream?" Write it down.

   _____

   _____

4. Ask the Holy Spirit to help you understand the meaning of your dream. Write down some ideas of what you think the dream *might* mean.

5. Identify how your heart bears witness to the different interpretation options.

6. What do you believe the dream is revealing? (Remember, dreams reveal; they don't condemn.)

7. Seek additional confirmation. If you believe you have received clarity on a dream, be sure to submit to several sources for review/evaluation first between acting upon it. Remember, never make a major decision in your life based only on a dream without receiving additional confirmation from the other ways that God speaks to us and guides us (peace in our hearts, the counsel of others, illumined Scriptures, God's still small voice, prophecy, anointed reasoning, etc.).

DREAM FROM DAY FOUR

1. Identify symbols in your dream (remember to see it from a symbolic perspective).

_____

_____

2. Because the symbols come from your life, ask yourself, "What does this symbol mean to me?"

_____

_____

3. Ask yourself, "What issue was I processing the day before I had the dream?" Write it down.

_____

_____

4. Ask the Holy Spirit to help you understand the meaning of your dream. Write down some ideas of what you think the dream *might* mean.

5. Identify how your heart bears witness to the different interpretation options.

6. What do you believe the dream is revealing? (Remember, dreams reveal; they don't condemn.)

7. Seek additional confirmation. If you believe you have received clarity on a dream, be sure to submit to several sources for review/evaluation first between acting upon it. Remember, never make a major decision in your life based only on a dream without receiving additional confirmation from the other ways that God speaks to us and guides us (peace in our hearts, the counsel of others, illumined Scriptures, God's still small voice, prophecy, anointed reasoning, etc.).

Dream from Day Five

1. Identify symbols in your dream (remember to see it from a symbolic perspective).

2. Because the symbols come from your life, ask yourself, "What does this symbol mean to me?"

3. Ask yourself, "What issue was I processing the day before I had the dream?" Write it down.

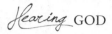

4. Ask the Holy Spirit to help you understand the meaning of your dream. Write down some ideas of what you think the dream *might* mean.

_____

_____

5. Identify how your heart bears witness to the different interpretation options.

_____

_____

6. What do you believe the dream is revealing? (Remember, dreams reveal; they don't condemn.)

_____

_____

7. Seek additional confirmation. If you believe you have received clarity on a dream, be sure to submit to several sources for review/evaluation first between acting upon it. Remember, never make a major decision in your life based only on a dream without receiving additional confirmation from the other ways that God speaks to us and guides us (peace in our hearts, the counsel of others, illumined Scriptures, God's still small voice, prophecy, anointed reasoning, etc.).

_____

_____

_____

_____

DREAM FROM DAY SIX

1. Identify symbols in your dream (remember to see it from a symbolic perspective).

   _____

   _____

2. Because the symbols come from your life, ask yourself, "What does this symbol mean to me?"

   _____

   _____

3. Ask yourself, "What issue was I processing the day before I had the dream?" Write it down.

   _____

   _____

4. Ask the Holy Spirit to help you understand the meaning of your dream. Write down some ideas of what you think the dream *might* mean.

5. Identify how your heart bears witness to the different interpretation options.

6. What do you believe the dream is revealing? (Remember, dreams reveal; they don't condemn.)

7. Seek additional confirmation. If you believe you have received clarity on a dream, be sure to submit to several sources for review/evaluation first between acting upon it. Remember, never make a major decision in your life based only on a dream without receiving additional confirmation from the other ways that God speaks to us and guides us (peace in our hearts, the counsel of others, illumined Scriptures, God's still small voice, prophecy, anointed reasoning, etc.).

DREAM FROM DAY SEVEN

1. Identify symbols in your dream (remember to see it from a symbolic perspective).

   ○ ▫ _____

   ○ ▫ _____

2. Because the symbols come from your life, ask yourself, "What does this symbol mean to me?"

   ○ ▫ _____

   ○ ▫ _____

3. Ask yourself, "What issue was I processing the day before I had the dream?" Write it down.

   ○ ▫ _____

   ○ ▫ _____

4. Ask the Holy Spirit to help you understand the meaning of your dream. Write down some ideas of what you think the dream *might* mean.

5. Identify how your heart bears witness to the different interpretation options.

6. What do you believe the dream is revealing? (Remember, dreams reveal; they don't condemn.)

7. Seek additional confirmation. If you believe you have received clarity on a dream, be sure to submit to several sources for review/evaluation first between acting upon it. Remember, never make a major decision in your life based only on a dream without receiving additional confirmation from the other ways that God speaks to us and guides us (peace in our hearts, the counsel of others, illumined Scriptures, God's still small voice, prophecy, anointed reasoning, etc.).

Dream Journal

Once you have finished going through this book, I recommend that you purchase an exclusive notebook for writing down and recording your dreams. If you want to explore dreams further, please visit our website (www.cwgministries.org) for books, DVDs, and free online videos available on *Hearing God through Your Dreams.*

In the meantime, we are going to provide you with several pages of lined writing space for recording them.

Dream Journal

About Mark and Patti Virkler

Mark Virkler, Ph.D. and Patti Virkler, D.Min. have co-authored more than 50 books in the areas of hearing God's voice and spiritual growth. They are the founders of Communion with God Ministries and Christian Leadership University, where the voice of God is at the center of every learning experience. Mark has taught on developing intimacy with God and spiritual healing for more than 30 years on six continents. The message has been translated into over 40 languages, and he has helped to establish more than 250 church-centered Bible schools around the world.

Ministry Information

You may feel led to host Mark Virkler in your community for a week-end seminar on "How to Hear God's Voice." Details can be found at:
www.cwgministries.org/seminars

Mark and Patti Virkler have written 60 books demonstrating how to take God's voice into area after area of life. These are available at:
www.cwgministries.org/catalog

They have also developed over 100 college courses for Christian Leadership University that put the voice of God in the center of your learning experience. These classes can all be taken from your home. View our complete catalog online at: **www.cluonline.com**

Would you allow the Virklers to recommend a coach to guide you in applying God's voice in every area of your life? Information about their Personal Spiritual Trainer program is available at:
www.cwgministries.org/pst

We invite you to become a certified facilitator of this course and teach others to hear God's voice! Find out the details at:
www.cwgministries.org/certified

Share your journaling, dreams and visions with others who have experienced this training! Healing rooms, prayer counseling rooms and dream interpretation discussion threads are also available. Thousands are gathering to share their lives at:
www.KoinoniaNetwork.org